DECID
FORESTS

ENDANGERED
BIOMES

DONNA LATHAM

Nomad Press
A division of Nomad Communications
10 9 8 7 6 5 4 3 2 1

Printed by Regal Printing Limited in China,
June 2010, Job Number 1005019
ISBN: 978-1-934670-54-5

Questions regarding the ordering of this book should be addressed to
Independent Publishers Group
814 N. Franklin St.
Chicago, IL 60610
www.ipgbook.com

Nomad Press
2456 Christian St.
White River Junction, VT 05001
www.nomadpress.net

Image Credits

corbisimages.com/ W. Cody, cover; Michael T. Sedam, i.

©iStockphoto.com/ Jan Rysavy, 1; Jussi Santaniemi, 1; AVTG, 3, 5; Mike
Bentley, 4, 11; Karin Mortimer, 5; Borut Trdina, 5; Ruud de Man, 6; Tamas Kooning
Lansbergen, 7; Don Nichols, 7; Alexander Takiev, 7; Luminis, 9; Živa Kirn, 9; Anna
Yu, 9; Nicholas Monu, 10; Valeria Titova, 12; German, 12; Jiri Vaclavek, 13; Eric
Isselée, 13, 15; Andy Gehrig, 13; Suzanne Carter, 14; Matthew Cole, 14; Vassiliy
Vishnevskiy, 14; VCH Images, 15; Vassiliy Vishnevskiy, 15; Jitalia17, 16; John
Pavel, 16; Marek Mnich, 16; luoman, 17; Doug Lloyd, 19; madcorona, 20; Nikada,
21; Tom Tietz, 22; Pawet Aniszewski, 24; Peter Mukherjee, 25; Randy Plett, 26.

CONTENTS

What Is a Biome?

Grab your backpack! You're about to embark on an exciting expedition to explore one of Earth's major **biomes**: the **deciduous** forest!

A biome is a large natural area with a distinctive **climate** and **geology**. The desert is a biome. The rainforest, ocean, and tundra are biomes. So is the deciduous forest. Biomes are the earth's communities.

Did You Know?

Scientists don't agree on how many biomes there are. Some divide the earth into five biomes. Others argue for 12.

Words to Know

biome: a large natural area with a distinctive climate, geology, and set of water resources. A biome's plants and animals are adapted for life there.

deciduous: describes trees and bushes that shed their leaves each year.

climate: average weather patterns in an area over a period of many years.

geology: the rocks, minerals, and physical structure of an area.

adapt: changes a plant or animal makes to survive in new or different conditions.

ecosystem: a community of living and nonliving things and their environment. Living things are plants, animals, and insects. Nonliving things are soil, rocks, and water.

environment: everything in nature, living and nonliving.

Each biome has its own biodiversity, which is the range of living things **adapted** for life there. It also contains many **ecosystems**. In an ecosystem, living and nonliving things interact with their **environment**.

Teamwork keeps the system balanced and working. Earth's biomes are connected together, creating a vast web of life.

2

Landscape and Climate

Trees, trees, and more trees define the **temperate** deciduous forest. Deciduous forests are one of the earth's most pleasant places, where humans have thrived for thousands of years.

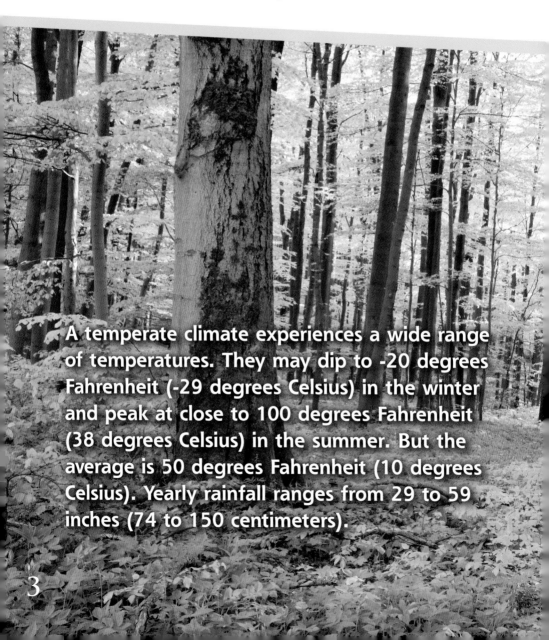

A temperate climate experiences a wide range of temperatures. They may dip to -20 degrees Fahrenheit (-29 degrees Celsius) in the winter and peak at close to 100 degrees Fahrenheit (38 degrees Celsius) in the summer. But the average is 50 degrees Fahrenheit (10 degrees Celsius). Yearly rainfall ranges from 29 to 59 inches (74 to 150 centimeters).

of the Deciduous Forest

You'll find temperate deciduous forests in the eastern United States, Canada, China, Japan, Russia, and central and eastern Europe. These areas are all in the **Northern Hemisphere**. There are a few, much smaller areas of deciduous forest in the **Southern Hemisphere**.

Words to Know

temperate: climate or weather that is not extreme.

Northern Hemisphere: the half of the planet north of the equator.

Southern Hemisphere: the half of the planet south of the equator.

Seasons characterize this biome. A cold winter follows a long, warm growing season of around six months. Temperate deciduous forests enjoy four seasons, each with its own weather. Snowy winters and hot summers are about the same length. Even with this dependable pattern, the length of each season can vary from year to year or from location to location.

fertile: good for growing plants.

nutrients: substances that organisms need to live and grow.

topsoil: top layer of soil.

organic matter: decaying plants and animals.

The soil in the deciduous forest biome is dark brown, **fertile**, and rich in **nutrients**. Plants and animals inhabit the ground level, or **topsoil**. Seeds sprout and plants take root in the blend of silt, sand, clay, and **organic matter**.

Did You Know?

Deciduous comes from the Latin word *decidere*, which means "to fall off." No wonder autumn is also called FALL.

Leaf litter, grasses, and other plants protect topsoil from getting too dry. When plants die, insects such as ants, spiders, centipedes, and termites chomp them up into teeny bits.

Decomposers also break down wastes and dead plants and animals, and recycle them into **humus**. Rich in nutrients, humus allows new plants to grow.

Below the topsoil is a layer called **subsoil**. Minerals and humus mingle together here. Thirsty roots push through sticky clay and weathered rocks searching for water sources.

Below the subsoil are layers of bedrock. Plant roots can't break through these deep layers of solid rock.

Words to Know

decomposers: bacteria, fungi, and worms that break down wastes and dead plants and animals.

humus: decaying organic matter made from dead plant and animal material.

subsoil: layer of soil below topsoil.

Plants Growing in the

Plants are the foundation of the **food chain**. They make their own food by capturing the sun's energy in a process called **photosynthesis**. Plants deliver the sun's energy to the animals and people who eat them.

The forest is divided into five main layers. On top, the forest **canopy** teems with the leafy branches of tall trees that capture as much sunlight as possible.

Broadleaf trees, including maples, oaks, and chestnut trees, extend up to 100 feet (30 meters) tall. They create a cover of shade across the forest like a giant patio umbrella.

Deciduous Forest Have Adapted

Words to Know

food chain: a community of animals and plants where each is eaten by another higher up in the chain.

photosynthesis: the process through which plants create food, using light as a source of energy.

canopy: an umbrella of trees over the forest.

The second layer is the **understory** of saplings, or young trees. Below the understory is the shrub layer, which contains shrubs and bushes, then the herb layer with herbs, short plants, and berries. The fifth layer is the forest floor, or carpet. Dark and chilly, the floor is covered with leaf litter.

Deciduous trees are well adapted to change with the seasons. During the fall as the days grow shorter, photosynthesis stops. **Chlorophyll**, which gives leaves their vivid green hues, breaks down.

After displaying their "fall colors" for a few weeks, trees drop their leaves to the forest floor to become next year's leaf litter.

Trees go **dormant** for the winter. Growth stops and vegetation sleeps away the frigid months. When the days grow longer and temperatures start to warm up in the spring, trees grow new leaves and start producing food again.

Words to Know

understory: the second layer of the forest, made up of saplings.

chlorophyll: a substance that makes plants green. Used in photosynthesis to capture light energy.

dormant: when plants are not actively growing during the winter.

Animals Living in the

Animals in the deciduous forest use different food sources. **Herbivores**, including deer, rabbits, beavers, and grasshoppers, munch only plants. **Omnivores**, such as skunks and wild boars, eat both plants and animals. **Carnivores** eat only other animals. These hunters include cougars, wolves, and owls.

Deciduous Forest Have Adapted

Slugs and worms are some of the decomposers that digest and break down dead leaves, plants, insects, and animals. They pass nutrients into the soil.

Animals in the deciduous forest have **adaptations** to seasonal changes. During autumn, many birds **migrate** south to warmer biomes. Some deciduous forest animals **hibernate** for the winter, while others make a few changes to their routines.

Words to Know

herbivore: an animal that eats only plants.

omnivore: an animal that eats both plants and animals.

carnivore: an animal that eats only other animals.

adaptation: the development of physical or behavioral changes to survive in an environment.

migrate: to move from one environment to another when seasons change.

hibernate: to sleep through the winter.

14

now: Least weasels have a brown and white coat for most of the year.

then: The least weasel sprouts a snow white coat for a winter disguise from **predators**. This **camouflage** hides the least weasel in the snow.

Squirrels pack on an extra 20 percent of their body weight to help them survive the harsh winter. Have you ever found a mound of acorns hidden under a bush? It may have been a secret squirrel stash to use during the winter.

Some animals, such as the meadow vole, live in the **subnivian zone** under the snow. Larger predators, such as coyotes, foxes, hawks, and owls **prey** on voles. With its powerful sense of hearing, coyotes listen to life underground. The coyote stops, tilts its head, and listens. Then the coyote pounces like a cat.

Animals adapt to their environment in other ways, too. A marsh is a freshwater wetland bordering lakes, ponds, and streams. Herons and cranes are two large birds that inhabit marshes. Demonstrating adaptation to the marsh, herons and cranes use their long legs to slosh through the shallow water in search of food.

Words to Know

predator: an animal that hunts another animal for food.

camouflage: colors or patterns that allow a plant or animal to blend in with its environment.

subnivian zone: the small open space between the snow and the ground.

prey: to hunt. Also animals hunted by other animals.

Environmental Threats

Acid rain may be today's greatest threat to the deciduous forest. Burning coal to generate electricity pollutes the air. Waste from cars and factories also pollutes the air. When this pollution mixes with water droplets in the air, it falls as acid rain. Acid rain is snow or rain with deposits of acid. This kind of rain injures leaves and weakens trees, slowing their growth and causing them to produce fewer seeds.

Climate change threatens every biome on our planet, including the deciduous forest. Burning fuels releases a gas called carbon dioxide into the air, which traps the sun's heat like a blanket around the earth. This is causing a rise in temperatures around the world, as well as more violent storms, flooding, droughts, and heat waves.

Climate change will alter the balance of the ecosystems.

Disease introduced by humans has destroyed trees in the deciduous forest. The chestnut blight came from Europe in 1904, and killed nearly every chestnut tree in America. Dutch elm disease reached the United States around 1930 on crates made with infected elm wood from Europe. Since then it has killed millions and millions of these enormous trees. Many towns have lost all of their elm trees.

Did You Know?

Coal plants making electricity in the southern and midwestern sections of the United States produce pollution that falls as acid rain the northeastern United States.

Biodiversity at Risk

When an animal or plant **species** becomes extinct, that means it's gone forever. Natural occurrences, such as volcanic eruptions, have caused **extinctions** in the past.

Today, animals may become extinct when people overhunt them or when their **habitats** or food sources are destroyed.

Words to Know

species: a type of animal or plant.

extinction: the death of an entire species so that it no longer exists.

habitat: a plant or animal's home.

invasive species: a plant or animal species that enters an ecosystem and spreads, harming the system's balance.

What Eats What?

The wolf is a predator at the top of the food chain, eating deer, beavers, and other animals that eat plants.

Sometimes, an **invasive species** disrupts the delicate balance of the local ecosystem.

The red wolf is native to the southeastern deciduous forest. Red wolves have been driven out of their habitat by humans and were hunted nearly to extinction. The red wolf was actually extinct in the wild by 1980, but was bred in captivity and reintroduced in the wild in North Carolina. Today there are about 100 red wolves living in the wild.

Path to Extinction

Rare: Only a small number of the species is alive. Scientists are concerned about the future of the species.

Threatened: The species lives, but its numbers will likely continue to decline. It will probably become endangered.

Endangered: The species is in danger of extinction in the very near future.

Extinct in the Wild: Some members of the species live, but only in protected captivity and not out in the wild.

Extinct: The species has completely died out. It has disappeared from the planet.

22

The Future of the

As with all of the earth's biomes, the threats to the deciduous forest are pressing. But there are signs of hope. Many people recognize the need to conserve and protect the deciduous forest. Planting a tree to replace every tree that is cut down is one way to help preserve this important biome.

National parks protect the natural beauty of many areas. The Great Smoky National Park in Tennessee and the Cape Breton Highlands National Park in Nova Scotia, Canada, are just two. The Appalachian Trail runs 2,175 miles (3,500 kilometers) from Georgia to Maine through temperate deciduous forests.

These are all areas that you can go to and enjoy the natural beauty of the deciduous forest.

Deciduous Forest

Conservation Challenge

Think about what you can do to benefit the environment. What actions can you take? How can you inspire others to do the same?

- Conserve paper. Paper is made from trees from the deciduous forest. And don't forget to recycle paper and newspapers. Paper or plastic? Neither! Bring a reusable bag when you go shopping.

- Conserve energy. More than half of the electricity used in the United States is generated by burning coal. Burning coal leads to climate change. So turn off the lights when you leave a room. Turn off the TV when you're done watching. These actions will also help reduce acid rain.

- Recycle those plastic water bottles. Recycling one plastic bottle will save as much energy as it takes to power a 60-watt light bulb for six hours. Better yet, fill a reusable container with water from the tap.

Glossary

acid rain: rain that contains pollution from burning fuels.

adapt: changes a plant or animal makes to survive in new or different conditions.

adaptation: the development of physical or behavioral changes to survive in an environment.

biodiversity: the range of living things in an ecosystem.

biome: a large natural area with a distinctive climate, geology, and set of water resources. A biome's plants and animals are adapted for life there.

camouflage: colors or patterns that allow a plant or animal to blend in with its environment.

canopy: an umbrella of trees over the forest.

carnivore: an animal that eats only other animals.

chlorophyll: a substance that makes plants green. Used in photosynthesis to capture light energy.

climate: average weather patterns in an area over a period of many years.

climate change: a change in the world's weather and climate.

deciduous: describes trees and bushes that shed their leaves each year.

decomposers: bacteria, fungi, and worms that break down wastes and dead plants and animals.

dormant: when plants are not actively growing during the winter.

ecosystem: a community of living and nonliving things and their environment. Living things are plants, animals, and insects. Nonliving things are soil, rocks, and water.

environment: everything in nature, living and nonliving.

extinction: the death of an entire species so that it no longer exists.

fertile: good for growing plants.